My 21 Day Prayer

WITH JOURNAL

FOR HEALING/RECOVERY

Kay M. Forde

WESTBOW
PRESS®
A DIVISION OF THOMAS NELSON
& ZONDERVAN

WestBow Press books may be ordered through booksellers or by contacting:

WestBow Press
A Division of Thomas Nelson & Zondervan
1663 Liberty Drive
Bloomington, IN 47403
www.westbowpress.com
844-714-3454

Interior Graphics/Art Credit: Kaylanie Douglas

Scripture taken from the King James Version of the Bible.

ISBN: 979-8-3850-3594-6 (sc)
ISBN: 979-8-3850-3595-3 (hc)
ISBN: 979-8-3850-3596-0 (e)

Print information available on the last page.

WestBow Press rev. date: 10/30/2024

Dedication

This book is dedicated to all those seeking solace, strength, healing, and recovery through prayer. May these 21 days be a transformative journey, bringing you closer to God and filling your heart with His peace and love. Remember you are never alone; God's boundless love and mercy are with you every step of the way.

To my family and friends, whose unwavering support and love has been my anchor, thank you for walking this path with me. Your faith and encouragement have been a constant source of inspiration.

Above all, to the Almighty, whose boundless grace and mercy make all things possible. May this book be a vessel of His love and a beacon of hope for all who turn its' pages. May your prayers be answered and your spirits uplifted.

In faith and gratitude,
Kay M. Forde

Preface

This book was developed to help patients' with life threatening diseases get through this journey trusting and believing that God will not fail them and he will grant total healing. It is a beacon of hope, a sanctuary where individuals, whether alone or in communion, can fix their gaze upon God and entrust their afflictions into His unwavering care. There are even a journal pages at the back of the book to make your own notes of your journey and connection with God.

Throughout this 21-day prayer journey, I encourage you to consider incorporating fasting as an essential part of your spiritual discipline. Fasting, when coupled with prayer, offers profound benefits and serves multiple purposes. It not only demonstrates the intensity and sincerity of your desire in prayer but also draws you closer to God. By fasting, you show God that you are serious enough about your prayer request to make a personal sacrifice. This act of devotion can deepen your spiritual connection and amplify the power of your prayers, making this journey even more transformative.

The genesis of these prayers stems from my own battle with cancer—a diagnosis that rattled the very foundations of my existence. At the age of thirty-six, confronted with the stark reality of a rare stage IV cancer diagnosis, I grappled with disbelief and despair. I had thought to myself, I have plans and things I wanted to accomplish. I did not believe I served my purpose here on earth yet. I did not want to accept it as my fate and I questioned God as to "Why me?" But after seeing different doctors and getting second and third opinions, I realized this was the journey I had to take. So I decided to just pour out my heart to God in prayer. Yet, amidst the turmoil, a family member said to me "have faith and trust God's process".

So after being told of my way forward with the treatment process, I got instructions from the Holy Spirit to do a 21 day prayer and fast before I began my first step, which was Chemotherapy. Also before I started the 21 days I was instructed to write down my prayers for each day. So each prayer is not the same as whatever was pressing upon my heart and mind, I lamented in prayer as well as put it in writing. Overall, these prayers asked almighty God for healing and recovery for the horrible disease of cancer. Also even though I was pouring my heart out each day and trying my hardest to hold onto faith, I still questioned God as to why me. But I was comforted and got an answer to my question at the end of 21 days. I heard a voice say to me "Why not you" and right there and then I knew I was to be a testimony for his glory.

This book is to encourage you and give you hope through prayer. To help you build or regain your faith and trust in Yeshua and his words, his promises over your life. You will find scriptures embedded in each prayer. Scriptures are used as God says his words doesn't return to him void. So in prayer we will remind him of all that was said to us. God's Word is a steadfast anchor in the tumultuous seas of life. As we lift our petitions before Him, we do so with the assurance that His promises endure, His wisdom surpasses our understanding, and His love transcends all earthly trials.

Scripture also aligns our request with God's will, guiding our hearts and minds to seek him and believe in his word and promises. As we come before him in prayer, humbly asking for help, healing, and full recovery, it is essential that we trust the process he has laid out for us. Proverbs 3:5 encourages us to "lean not on our own understanding," reminding us that our perspective is limited and often clouded by fear and doubt. Instead, we are called to place our trust entirely in God, recognizing that His wisdom far surpasses our own.

We find profound comfort in the knowledge that God's "thoughts are higher than our thoughts" and his ways are beyond our comprehension (Isaiah 55:8-9). This assurance allows us to surrender our anxieties and uncertainties, knowing that he is in control and that his plans for us are rooted in love and goodness. Even when we cannot see the bigger picture, we can rest in the confidence that God's intentions are always for our ultimate benefit.

I believe these prayers are simple yet powerful. They will give each person, courage each day, that they are focusing their eyes on God and trusting that he is a miracle worker and great physician. Each prayer will help you communicate with Yeshua on a deeper level, that your level of fear is reduced, knowing that no matter what, God has the best interest for you and those around you. This book will help elevate your prayer life, spiritual life and spiritual knowledge on scriptures that are used to bring healing and restoration.

Lastly, as a cancer survivor, I pray this book serves as a testament to the transformative power of prayer, an instrument of encouragement, and a beacon of hope for all who traverse the shadowed valleys of illnesses. May these prayers serve as a conduit for divine healing, a source of spiritual fortitude, and a testament to the boundless mercy of our Heavenly Father. As you embark on this journey of faith, may you find comfort in the knowledge that you are held in the palm of His hand, and that His plans for you are plans for good, to give you a future and hope.

With faith and gratitude,
Kay M. Forde

Acknowledgements

I would like to express my sincere gratitude to all those who have contributed to the creation and publication of this 21-day prayer book for those diagnosed with a life threatening illnesses and physical challenges. This project has been a labor of love, and it would not have been possible without the unwavering support, encouragement, and contributions of many individuals. Their support and prayers have been invaluable in sustaining me when I went through my own challenge of battling cancer.

First and foremost, I am deeply thankful to the Almighty for providing me with the inspiration, strength, comfort and guidance throughout this journey. His presence has been a constant source of encouragement and direction. It is through his divine intervention that the formation of this book was influenced and brought to life. It intends offer solace and strength to those facing the hardest battles of their lives. Without his grace and unfailing love, this book would not have been possible. Every page has scriptures to remind you of his word and a reflection of His endless compassion and mercy.

Secondly, I will like to thank my amazing husband who has supported and encouraged me to get this book written and published. He never left my side through it all. Also special thanks to all my loving family, particularly my mom, my dad, Ashmin and Simmonne who were physically there with me every step of the way. In addition, I must mention my loving and faithful pastors, Pastor Paul Bachew of Faith Assembly International and Pastor Selwyn Jagdeo of The Assembly of God. I know you bruised your knees for God's mighty hand to be over me and bring healing to my body. Furthermore, I must express thank you to all of my caring friends, particularly Mrs. Lewis, Ria Ginga, Andrea, Stacy, Shelly Anne, Isidora, Nurse Annamarie and the Sent One family. You have all stood in the gap as prayer warriors from day one and gave support in your own special way.

I am also grateful to Dr. S. Medford, ENT Specialist at Gulf View Medical Centre for performing a smooth, successful and satisfactory surgery. To the other doctors, medical professionals, caregivers, and support network at SWRHA hospital who worked tirelessly to provide care, comfort, and encouragement to me, thank you. To Dr. A. Guerra, a phenomenal Consultant Oncologist at National Radiotherapy Centre, thank you for being kind and compassionate and being a beacon of hope and encouragement to me and all other cancer patients. You are a gem and I am grateful to have met you and to be under your care from inception. Another great person that I must mention is Dr. M. Kumar, Clinical Oncologist at SMC Southern Medical Specialist Hospital, your compassion and dedication make a profound difference in the lives of so many.

Lastly, I would like to thank the readers for embracing this book and incorporating these prayers into your life. You are powerful prayers grounded in faith, believing that God is capable and willing to respond. I hope that these prayers bring comfort, strength, and hope to all those who are seeking restoration of their health and full recovery from their life threatening disease. Know that God's will, will always be done and trusting in his wisdom, timing, and power is essential. Believing while you pray and holding on to faith, will make you strong mentally and help you get through your trying time.

Thank you once again to everyone who has contributed and supported me in their own special way through my journey. I love you and appreciate you and even though your name was not mentioned, know that I do acknowledge the part you played in helping me during my trying time. Your prayers, kindness, generosity and support are deeply appreciated.

With love and gratitude,
Kay M. Forde

Scriptures

Proverbs 3:5-6:
Trust in the Lord with all your heart and lean not on
your own understanding; in all your ways submit to
him, and he will make your paths straight.

Ephesians 6:12
For we do not wrestle against flesh and blood, but against the rulers,
against the authorities, against the cosmic powers over this present
darkness, against the spiritual forces of evil in the heavenly places.

Hebrews 4:12
For the word of God is living and active, sharper than any two-edged
sword, piercing to the division of soul and of spirit, of joints and of
marrow, and discerning the thoughts and intentions of the heart.

Jeremiah 29:11
"For I know the plans I have for you," declares the Lord, "plans
for welfare and not for evil, to give you a future and a hope."

Jeremiah 17:14
Heal me, LORD, and I'll be healed. Save me and
I'll be saved, for you are my heart's desire.

Contents

Sovereign Lord,

As I stand on the threshold of this 21-day journey of prayer and faith, I humbly come before you, acknowledging my need for your divine guidance and strength. I am aware that this journey is not one I can undertake alone, and so I seek your presence to be with me every step of the way. Lord, prepare my heart to be receptive to your voice, my mind to comprehend the depth of your wisdom, and my spirit to be attuned to your divine will. All help me to deeply trust in your sovereign power.

Father, you are the Great Healer, the one who mends our broken bodies and spirits, the Provider of peace that surpasses all understanding, and the Shepherd who faithfully guides us through every valley of shadow and doubt. As I embark on this path of focused prayer, dedicating these 21 days to seek your face, I ask you to root my heart firmly in the truth of your promises. Let your word be the foundation, unshakable and secure. May your presence be obvious, your comfort undeniable, and your strength ever-present as I journey through this season of prayer.

Lord, I acknowledge the uncertainty and the shadows cast by the illness, but I choose to fix my eyes on you, the Author and Finisher of my faith. Strengthen my belief in your ability to heal and restore, reminding me that you are Jehovah Rapha, the Lord who heals. Let my hope be up held by the certainty that nothing is impossible with you and that your love for me is steadfast and unchanging.

Fill me with Your Holy Spirit that I may be reminded of your presence every step of the way. Let Your Word be a lamp unto my feet and a light unto my path, illuminating my journey with hope and clarity. May each day of this prayer journey draw me closer to you, deepening my understanding and reliance on your love and power.

Lord, I pray for healing, not just of the body, but also of the mind and spirit. May this time of prayer be a sanctuary, a place where I can lay down my fears and weariness and take up your rest and peace. Let your will be done in my life as it is in heaven, and may I emerge from this journey transformed and renewed by your loving touch.

Thank you, Father, for the assurance that you hear every prayer. I trust in your timing and your perfect plan. May these next 21 days be a testament to your faithfulness and a declaration of my faith in you.

In Jesus' Name, I pray, Amen.

Day 1

REPENTANCE AND FORGIVENESS

Eternal Lord,

Today, I come before you with a heart seeking forgiveness and renewal. I recognize that there have been times when I have failed to persist in the paths you have set for me. Reflecting on your word in 1 John 1:9, I am comforted by your promise that if we confess our sins, you are faithful and just to forgive us our sins and to cleanse us from all unrighteousness. So Lord, I confess my moments of weakness and disobedience.

I acknowledge my imperfections and the ways I have fallen short of your glory. I repent of my sins, asking for your cleansing and renewal. I confess and renounce any sin and unknown agreements with darkness, which may be blocking your promises for deliverance and healing. Forgive me, God. Cleanse my heart and renew a right spirit within me.

Father, I desire to embody the perseverance and dedication of Jesus. From this moment, I choose to submit fully to the lordship of Christ, allowing His example to guide my every action and decision. I ask you to cultivate within me the fruits of the Spirit: patience, faithfulness, and a spirit of enduring resilience.

Lord, I declare that from this day forward, I will not quit and I will, conquer this thing. I am determined to face the challenges laid before me, especially this battle with (name your illness). Like Jesus, who set His face like flint towards Jerusalem, I too set my heart and mind to obey and trust you—no matter the obstacles I encounter. Your strength is made perfect in my weakness.

I pray for your divine intervention in my life. Help me, Lord, to hold onto my faith without feeling disgraced or ashamed. Make evident your strength and mercy in my circumstances. Let those around me see your hand at work and know that you are a God of salvation and healing. Lord, show me favor; I hope in you. Be my strength every morning, my salvation in times of distress. (Isaiah 33:2)

I stand firmly on your promises, trusting in your boundless power to heal and preserve my life. I release any lingering guilt and shame, embracing the freedom and newness of life that comes from your grace. Thank You, Lord, for your unwavering favor and the hope found in Jesus Christ. Your sacrifice on the cross has made a way for me to be reconciled to you, and I am eternally grateful.

Thank you, Lord, for hearing my prayer. I praise you for the miracles yet to come for nothing is impossible for you.

In Jesus' Name, I pray, Amen.

DAY 1

AFFIRMATION

I am strong in spirit, mind, and body.

Day 2

DIVINE INTERVENTION AND FAVOR

Lord Almighty,

In this challenging time, I come before you with a heavy heart but full of faith. As I navigate through this trial, I beseech you to be my constant companion. Show me your presence, reassure me with your love, and fortify my spirit. Lord, I pray for your divine intervention to quell the works of the enemy and restore my health. In the powerful name of Jesus, I ask you to bring about healing and peace within me. Have mercy on me, Lord, because I'm frail. Heal me, Lord, because my bones are shaking in terror! *(Psalm 6:2)*

Today, I am reminded of your words in Philippians 4:6—to be anxious for nothing but in everything, through prayer and supplication with thanksgiving, to let my requests be known to you. On this day, [state the date and time], I am committing to praying fervently for the full 21 days, believing wholeheartedly in the attaining answered prayers. Each day, I will lift my voice in praise, confident that you are already at work in my life bringing about healing, restoration, and blessings beyond measure.

I place my trust in your promises, believing in a bright and blessed future. You will be my peace in the midst of this storm as scripture proves, I am confident you can heal and you can bring life and restoration. I ask You, Lord, to open the doors that lead to abundance and favor, as proclaimed in Isaiah 45:1-3. Dear God, touch me from the crown of my head to the sole of my feet. Shower upon me blessings, favor, mercy, grace and victory over this sickness, for you know me by name and have called me for a purpose.

I recall your promise that when the enemy comes in like a flood, the Holy Spirit will raise a standard against him. (Isaiah 59:19) Lord, in the mighty name of Jesus, I declare your divine protection and guidance over me, helping me to maintain my faith and level of anxiety through this trying time. Help me to stand firm, anchored in your peace as it surpasses all understanding.

Father, I thank you in advance for your unfailing love, favor and the miracle of healing that I believe you will grant me. May your presence be profoundly evident in my life as you show up and show your power in magnificent ways? You are my healer and my friend and I will trust in your mercies that are new every day.

Thank you, Lord, for hearing my prayers.

Amen.

DAY 2

AFFIRMATION

I walk in divine health and strength

Day 3

RESTORATION, GUIDANCE, AND DIVINE VICTORY

Loving Father,

I lean on your comforting presence and guidance. I declare victory over the plots of the enemy and liberation from all bondages. Please make your presence unmistakably clear to me, light my path, and reassure me with the steadfastness of your protection and guidance. I ask that you disrupt and destroy the plots of the enemy, liberate me from any bondage, and restore my health in the mighty name of Jesus.

Dear God I give my burdens to you as I am confident I still have the bright future you have planned for me. I pray Psalm 23; yea though I walk through the valley of death I will fear no evil, for you are with me. Your rod and your staff will comfort me and protect me. I declare that you are my healer and protector, and I trust in your power to overcome every obstacle and restore my health. Supernaturally touch my life O, God; I know this is not too hard for you. I know you are able to do exceedingly and abundantly above all I can ever ask.

You know me intimately, Lord. You have known me from the moment I was formed in my mother's womb, and you have called me by name, acknowledging me as your beloved child. Every thought, every fear, every joy I experience is known to you. Today, I ask for an expression of your love in a significant way. Show up in my life with your miraculous power, granting me the healing miracle I seek and the victories you have promised.

Thank you for your enduring faithfulness and boundless love. Your blessings are pure and bring no sorrow with them, and I am deeply grateful for your merciful kindness that never ceases. Proverbs 10:22; Lamentations 3:22-23) With a heart overflowing with gratitude, I will continue to recount all your wonderful deeds and celebrate your goodness in my life, just as it is expressed in Psalm 9:1.

Lord, as I walk through this challenging trial, I pray that your glory becomes evident in every aspect of my life. May I see your hand in every victory and feel your presence continuously guiding me. You are my refuge, a strong tower in times of trouble and a place where I am protected and fortified against all adversities.

Thank you, Lord, for your unwavering support and for allowing me to live under an Open Heaven where I can receive miracles which I believe are on their way. Your power and grace sustain me, and I am confident that your promises will be fulfilled.

I place my full trust in you. Amen.

DAY 3
AFFIRMATION

God's power is restoring my health.

Day 4

DIVINE PROTECTION AND VICTORY UNDER GOD'S COVENANT

Dear Lord,

I stand firm under the covenant you made with Abraham, assured that I inherit all the promises and privileges you extended to Israel, as proclaimed in Isaiah 45:17. I come before you again on this new day, in my time of need, seeking your mercies, divine protection and the victory of healing, for I acknowledge my help solely comes from you.

I know you are my refuge and my fortress, my steadfast place of trust. In moments of distress, I turn to You, O Lord, believing in your promise that those who seek you will lack no good thing (Psalm 34:10). I hold on to your word that all things work together for good to those who love you (Romans 8:28). My love for you is unwavering, Lord, as you have shown your steadfast love to me time and time again.

Lord, I boldly declare restoration as these challenges and adversities were foreseen by you, and I trust in your plan. According to Isaiah 54:17, no weapon forged against me shall prevail, and you will refute every tongue that accuses me. You are my hiding place; shielding me from trouble and surrounding me in songs of deliverance so I can be an over comer, a survivor and live to testify of your greatness. (Psalm 32:7-8).

I decree and declare that you will continue to contend with those who secretly plot against me. Expose the falsehoods and reveal the malevolent intents aimed at me so I can be more specific in my prayers. Grant me victory despite any negative or evil thoughts and deeds, for you are my strength and my redeemer. Affirm my righteousness that is only made possible through Christ, that all may see your hand in my life.

Thank you, Lord, for the assurance of your deliverance. You, the omniscient and Almighty, know all things. I remind you of your promise that when the enemy comes in like a flood, the Holy Spirit will raise a standard against him. I implore you, in the name of Jesus, to raise your battle standard, protecting me, your child.

Lord, I believe and declare your angels are fully equipped to battle on my behalf, safeguarding my life and restoring my health. I thank you in advance for my deliverance and healing, knowing that with you, no weapon formed against me shall prosper. Your victory is certain, and in that, I place my trust and hope.

By the blood of Jesus, I plead for protection and deliverance. Amen.

DAY 4

AFFIRMATION

God's healing light fills every part of my being.

Day 5

MERCY AND RESTORATION

Father God,

Your steadfast love never ceases, and your mercies never come to an end. They are new every morning; great is your faithfulness. As proclaimed in Lamentations 3:22-23, your unwavering love and boundless compassion are a daily reminder of your eternal faithfulness and grace.

Lord, today I seek your mercy and divine intervention and powerful healing. Deliver me, O Lord, from the hands of those who intend harm and from circumstances that threaten my wellbeing. If surgery is necessary, I pray that you guide the hands of the medical professionals, granting them wisdom and skill to perform with excellence to ensure my life is preserved. I also pray my recovery time is swift and smooth. May my body heal quickly and completely, free from any complications and ensure my health is restored.

But in the meantime I pray for your boundless mercy and endless compassion as I humbly seek your healing touch. May I not lose hope or falter in faith, but instead, find solace in your loving embrace. Guide me in your wisdom, O Lord, and lead me on the path of healing and renewal. Pour out your grace upon me and grant me the strength to endure this trial. Let your mercy surround me like a gentle embrace, bringing comfort and peace to my troubled heart and mind.

In all of this I stand firm on your word and claim the promises you have made. You are the God who forgives our sins and heals our diseases. Your mercy knows no bounds, and your grace is sufficient for us. Your light breaks forth like the dawn, illuminating our path with hope and restoration. Your righteousness goes before us, and your glory surrounds us, shielding us from harm.

I trust in your promises, O Lord, with unwavering confidence, knowing that you are faithful to fulfill every word spoken over me. May your presence be my constant companion, a divine light that illuminates my path, guiding me through the darkest valleys. Lift me up on wings like eagles, giving me support and strength to soar above this storm.

Lord, in your boundless loving kindness and mercy, I humbly come before you and ask that you hear my heartfelt prayer. As your beloved child, I seek the fullness of your mercy and the restorative power of your grace in my life. I am in need of your healing touch and the renewal that only you can bring. Show me your mighty works and let me live to testify of your endless goodness.

Strengthen my faith and deepen my reliance on your unfailing love. I commit to placing my complete trust in you. I proclaim and affirm healing over my body.

In the powerful name of Jesus, I pray. Amen.

DAY 5

AFFIRMATION

I am surrounded by God's love and compassion.

Day 6

HEALING AND DIVINE DEMONSTRATION OF GRACE

O Lord God,

I come before you acknowledging your sovereignty and the mighty name of Jesus, under which I claim victory and healing. You are the divine physician and know every cell in my body that is corrupted and not strong enough to fight. Begin healing every cell oh God that has made my body weak. In 2 Corinthians 12:9, you remind us that your grace is sufficient and that your power is perfected in my weakness. Lord, I am grateful for this unending grace that not only saves but sustains me daily.

Father, in this moment of physical weakness and illness, I do not accept this condition as my fate, for it is not reflective of your will. Lord, strip this ailment from my body and life, for in my own strength, I falter; yet through your authority and might, I am fortified and whole. I am nothing without you God, I am only complete in Christ. I pray now for a palpable increase of your grace in my life. May it propel every aspect of my existence, making the impossible possible, and filling my days with your miraculous works.

Lord, today I stand in faith for the evidence of miracles in my life—miracles that only your hand can perform. Bring forth new opportunities, new blessings, and new victories as you transform my trials into testimonies of your goodness and mercy. I declare that this sickness is not a barrier to the plans for me and, by your power, so I bind and cast out the sickness of (name the illness) from my body. In Jesus Name.

Let me see the tangible answers to my prayers, and experience life in its fullest measure as promised in John 10:10. I trust in your provision and thank you in advance for the abundant blessings you have prepared for me. Your grace is my shield and sustainer, and I look forward to witnessing your power at work in my life.

Perform wonders and work miracles that only you can do. Manifest your miraculous power in my life today, O God, and bring forth new wine out of me. Let your grace flow abundantly, healing me in every way. By your boundless mercy and love, I believe you will restore me completely.

Thank You, Father, for hearing my prayers and moving on my behalf. I await with expectation the great things you will do, knowing that all will be done for your glory.

In Jesus' Name, Amen.

DAY 6

AFFIRMATION

I trust in God's plan for my complete recovery.

Day 7

ANGELIC SHELTER AND DIVINE SHIELDING

Abba Father,

I come before you today seeking refuge and protection as promised in Psalm 91:1, where it is written that those who dwell in the secret place of the Most High shall abide under the shadow of the Almighty. My desire is to reside in that sacred shelter, O Lord, where your presence shields me and your power heals me. As I seek healing from this illness, I ask that you cover me with your mighty wings and provide me with the strength and courage to endure this trial.

In this moment of vulnerability, I place my complete trust in you, knowing that you are the Great Physician who can restore my health. I ask for your divine intervention to touch every part of my body, removing all afflictions and bringing me to a state of perfect well-being. Let your healing light penetrate every cell, every tissue, and every organ, revitalizing me from within.

Lord, as you have sent angels to assist, deliver, and minister to your servants in the scriptures—like Elijah, Peter, and even your Son, Jesus - I humbly request the same divine intervention in my life. Father, I ask that your angels bring forth messages of guidance and reassurance; provide protection and deliverance and strengthen me in times of weakness. May they also bring provisions and the resources I need from your heavenly supplies, as you are a God who provides abundantly for your children.

As I recognize that my battle is not against flesh and blood, but against the spiritual forces of evil in the heavenly realms, I take a stand in the authority given to me through Christ Jesus. I bind every spirit of darkness coming against me, nullifying their power and rendering their schemes ineffective. Lord, I humbly ask that you loose your mighty warring angels to engage in spiritual warfare on my behalf, surrounding me with your divine protection and strength.

Grant me, O Lord, the discernment to test the spirits I encounter, ensuring they are from you and carry the holiness and purity of your kingdom. Help me to recognize and understand the presence of your angels in my life, as those in the Bible did. Strengthen my spiritual senses so that I may perceive and appreciate the countless ways you respond to my prayers.

Father thank you for increasing my angelic support and for the countless ways you made visible your love and care in my life. I trust in your continuous protection and provision, confident in your promise to never leave nor forsake those who call on your name.

In the mighty and matchless name Jesus Christ, Amen.

DAY 7

AFFIRMATION

Every cell in my body is rejuvenated by God's grace.

Day 8

PERFECT PEACE AND PROPER ORDER

Heavenly Father,

In observance to your word in 1 Corinthians 14:40, I acknowledge you as the God of peace, not of confusion. You orchestrate all things decently and in order. Today, I submit the areas of my life that are held up in confusion and disorder under your sovereign Lordship. I surrender all areas to your divine wisdom and perfect plan. I recognize that the battles I face are not mine but yours, and I trust and declare you will bring peace and divine order.

Lord, I am faced with significant challenges, specifically in the areas of ------ and ------. These situations have brought confusion and disruption into my life. So I humbly ask you Father, where there is chaos bring clarity and where there is disorder bring structured guidance. May you grant me peace that surpasses all understanding during this time as I seek victory over these trials and health to continue fulfilling the purpose you have set for me.

God, I ask you to bring order from chaos. I speak to every disordered aspect of my life, commanding them in your mighty name to realign with your will — show up as healing, victory, joy, and prosperity. You are greater than any difficulty I might encounter, and I place my complete trust in your power to deliver me from all chaos and removing all afflictions and bringing me to a state of perfect well-being.

Lord, fill me with your power and presence, guiding me in this battle. Let your Holy Spirit continuously anoint me with the peace, health and the strength necessary to overcome. As declared in Psalm 119:133, order my steps oh God, by your will, today and forever more. Reestablish order in my life—remove sickness, resolve my debts, enhance my financial standing, and straighten any crooked paths. Shower me with your favor and mercy.

Father, continue to demonstrate your love for me and answer my prayers. Bring tranquility to any chaos around me and restore my peace of mind. Thank you for your faithfulness and for the assurance that you are always with me. May my victory over this illness be certain and inscribed in your Book of Life.

Today, I declare, with unwavering faith and firm resolve, that I will receive healing over my body and a complete recovery from all ailments and afflictions. I stand against every force that seeks to hinder my well-being, tearing down every stronghold that has taken root in my life.

I call upon the resurrection power of Jesus Christ to flow through my body.

In Jesus' name I pray, Amen.

DAY 8

AFFIRMATION

My faith in God brings me peace and strength.

Day 9

DIVINE INTERVENTION IN
TIMES OF AFFLICTION

Divine Healer,

I come before you today with a heart overflowing with love and gratitude. Your wisdom surpasses all understanding, and your love transcends even the deepest bonds I hold with family or friends. I thank You, Lord, for always being my defender and my shield, protecting me from harm and guiding me through every storm.

Thank You for the transformative work you are doing in my life, refining and purifying me through these trials. As it is written in Isaiah 48:10, you have chosen to refine me in the furnace of affliction. I recognize that these challenges are drawing me closer to you, molding and shaping me more into the likeness of Christ. In this refining process, I find solace and strength, knowing that your purpose is to bring out the best in me and to lead me to a deeper relationship with you.

Lord, I am grateful for your unending mercy and grace that sustain me daily. Your love and faithfulness never fail, and I am humbled by your continual presence in my life. As I navigate through these difficulties, I trust in your divine plan and the perfect timing of your interventions. I surrender my fears and anxieties to you, knowing that you hold my future securely in your hands.

I declare victory through Jesus Christ, who overcame all the powers of darkness. I plead the precious blood of Jesus over every circumstance of my life, both known and unknown. Let His sanctifying blood target and eradicate every free radical cell, preventing their further destruction. I claim the victory and peace that Christ secured through His sacrifice.

Lord, obliterate any attack on my life by the enemy, and break every yoke of bondage and affliction. As promised in Nahum 1:12-13, I believe you will shatter the yoke binding me and bring freedom to my life. I stand on your word that promises no more afflictions, trusting that you will bring me into a state of perfect peace and wholeness—shalom—where there is nothing lacking or broken.

Thank you, Father, for your unfailing love that wraps me close every day and your mighty power that sustains me through every trial. I am profoundly grateful for your constant protection and for the healing you will bring into my life, both physically and spiritually.

Bless my life, Oh God, in every aspect, so it reflects your boundless mercy and unmatched strength. Let my journey be a testament to your boundless mercy and unmatched strength.

In Jesus mighty Name, Amen.

DAY 9

AFFIRMATION

God's love surrounds and heals me.

Day 10

TRUSTING IN THE LORD'S DELIVERANCE

O God of my Salvation,

Thank You for being my unshakable Rock, my steadfast Shield, my impenetrable Defense, and my towering Stronghold. Each time I face obstacles, you create pathways where none seemed to exist, proving time and time again of your unwavering faithfulness. You have never failed me, and my trust in you remains unyielded.

I find solace in the secret place of the Most High, taking refuge under your wings as promised in Psalm 91:1. In this place of spiritual safety, protect me from all adversarial forces and let me witness the salvation you have prepared for me. Just as it is written in Exodus 14:13-19, where you delivered the Israelites from the Egyptians, I believe I will see this affliction, this illness, vanish and never to return. So I boldly declare and confirm healing over my body and spirit.

Lord, infuse my heart with your perfect love, casting out all fear, enabling me to rest wholly in you. In my weakness, your strength is made perfect, and I am reminded that apart from You, I can do nothing. Yet through Christ, all things are possible—including the peace that surpasses all understanding.

Help me to diligently put on and maintain the full armor of God (Ephesians 6:10-18), so I may stand firm against the schemes of the devil and secure the victory you have promised. In the authority given to me by Jesus Christ, I bind and cast out every spirit of infirmity, sickness, and disease attacking my body. Bring me through this trial with a testimony of total and complete healing—a victory like none I've ever experienced.

Lord, I know your angelic army is fighting on my behalf in the unseen realms, securing the triumph of your will in my life. I place my unwavering trust in you, for "in the Lord Jehovah is everlasting strength" (Isaiah 26:4). No matter the challenges you will carry me through.

I come humbly oh God, asking you to take up every battle in my life, especially this fight against (name your illness). As I stand still, because I know you are God, I want to witness your mighty hand at work, unshaken by the storms around me. Shield my life, preserve my health, and deliver me from this bodily disorder.

Thank You for Your mighty works, seen and unseen. I trust in your power to deliver me and restore my health completely. Let your miraculous works be evident in my life, and may your name be glorified through my testimony.

In Jesus mighty name, Amen.

DAY 10

AFFIRMATION

I release all fear and embrace God's healing power.

Day 11

DELIVERANCE AND HEALING

O Gracious God,

Today, my heart reaches out to you with a mixture of trust and yearning. While I have unwavering faith in your sovereignty and goodness, my current circumstances have, at times, caused me to drift from remembering your promises. I thus ask to see firmly, the blessings you have promised, as stated in Deuteronomy 28:2-14. I stand ready and open to receive them.

You are a God of mercy and grace, slow to anger and rich in love. I thank you for each new day, and having the breath of life. It is an opportunity to experience your transformative power, healing touch and receive deliverance from the chains that bind us. It also reminds me of your steadfast love, mercy and kindness.

Today, I bring before you my health struggles, specifically this battle with (name your illness). Your compassion towards your children is unending and it moves you to act. In this vain, I humbly ask for your profound mercy in my current situation. As I face the prospects of surgery and rigorous medication; hold me in your warm embrace and comfort me. Let each step in this journey contribute to a successful treatment, healing and the total recovery of my body.

Lord, in all things, I continue to seek your mercy and favor. Cleanse me from all unrighteousness and deliver me from this affliction. Your word promises deliverance and healing, and I hold onto these truths with all my might, for I believe in your word. So with the authority given by Christ, I cast out every unclean spirit and command them to leave and never return.

May your mercy flow abundantly, shielding me, guiding the doctors and health care personnel, and providing me with the strength to endure this trial. Let your healing power be apparent in my life, proving once again that you are a God who saves and restores. I believe you are the great and mighty God that still sits on the throne and performs miracles.

Thank You, Father, for your unending love and for deliverance and healing. I trust in your promises and await the fulfillment of your word in my life. Your faithfulness endures forever, and I hold onto your truth with a heart full of gratitude and hope.

Today I speak and establish by authority the freedom that Jesus won on the cross, as he declared that whom the Son sets free is free indeed.

Amen.

God's promises of health and wholeness
are manifesting in my life.

Day 12

THANKSGIVING AND COMMITMENT

Dear Heavenly Father,

Today, I come before you with a heart full of gratitude, recognizing how you've deemed me precious in your sight. Thank You for choosing me to showcase your glory, making my life a testament to your miraculous power. Even in my darkest times, you are the light that guides and sustains me.

I am reminded today by Hebrews 10:35-36 that I should not cast away my confidence, for it will be richly rewarded. You call for patience, that after I have done your will, I might receive your promises. Therefore, in this time of sickness, my desire is to steadfastly do your will. Despite the doctors' diagnoses, I choose to live righteously and uphold your decrees, that I might see your glory significantly noticeable in my life.

Lord, your report is the one I believe above all others for I know you are the great physician. As I walk this path of healing, I will sing of your goodness and declare your praises. Your presence brings peace and comfort, and I find refuge under your wings. Psalm 91:4 says, "He will cover you with his feathers, and under his wings you will find refuge; his faithfulness will be your shield and rampart."

I pledge to glorify your name repeatedly, proclaiming that salvation, glory, and power belong to you as revealed in Revelation 19:1. Your presence envelops me, offering strength and hope each day. Your strength sustains me, and your hope fills my heart. I trust in your promises and rely on your unfailing love. In moments of weakness, you are my rock and my refuge. Your grace is sufficient for me, and your power is made perfect in my weakness. 2 Corinthians 12:9

Father, I commit to proclaiming your name and sharing the good news of your salvation. May my life be a testimony to your glory and power. Let every word I speak and every action I take reflect your love and grace. I thank you for the blessings you have poured into my life and for the assurance of your eternal presence.

Thank you Father for considering me worthy, to be an example of your endless mercy, grace and power. May my life continually reflect your love and serve as a beacon of faith to others.

In the precious name of Jesus, I offer my thanks and commit my path to you.

Amen.

DAY 12
AFFIRMATION

God's mercy renews my strength each day.

Day 13

RESTORATION AND GRATITUDE

God Almighty,

Today, I come before you with a heart full of hope, seeking your divine intervention. I humbly ask you to reveal the answers to my prayers and fill my heart with overwhelming joy as I trust in your promise of restoration. Father God, I sincerely pray for your divine provision in my life. Restore my health to what it was before this illness struck, or even better, as I know your power has no bounds.

As your word said in 3 John 1:2 "Beloved, I pray that in every way you may prosper and enjoy good health, as your soul also prospers." So Lord I pray for holistic health – body, soul, and spirit. Let your healing flow through every part of me. I declare your promises over my life, believing in the power of your word. I praise you, Lord, and thank you for the healing that is already at work within me.

Lord, let the wealth of your roar at this critical time elevate my circumstances and yield positive results. According to your promise, may the wealth of the roar turn towards me right now! Jesus, Lion of Judah, roar mightily over these free radical cells that roam my body. Instill fear in them and cause them to miraculously disappear and may the good cells reign supreme.

Lord, split the sea of sickness for me, so that I may walk through it safely. I declare that you will rescue me, so I will make it to the other side and stand to praise your name. I am grateful to be your child, worthy of receiving your mercy and a second chance at life. Dear Lord as you said in Jeremiah 30:17: "But I will restore you to health and heal your wounds,"

I decree and declare your words shall not return to you void and it shall be fulfilled in my life.

Help me, Father, to always be mindful of your presence and acts of kindness. I do not want to take for granted all that you have done for me. I thank you for your favor, which endures forever. As your word said in Psalm 103:2-3: "Praise the Lord, my soul, and forget not all his benefits—who forgives all your sins and heals all your diseases." May I always remember to acknowledge every blessing you have ever poured into my life that I may receive healing from my illness.

Thank you, Lord, for hearing my prayer. Your attentive ear and compassionate heart are a constant source of comfort and reassurance to me.

I declare full restoration of my health. In the mighty name of Jesus, I pray.

Amen.

DAY 13
AFFIRMATION

My mind is clear, and my body is healthy.

Day 14

REST, HEALING AND STRENGTH

Merciful Father,

Your Word invites us to come to Jesus when we are weary and burdened, promising us rest. I cling to this promise today, Lord, as I feel the weight of my trials. Jeremiah 17:14 resonates deeply with me: "Heal me, O Lord, and I shall be healed; save me, and I shall be saved, for you are my praise." Lord, I rely on the power of Your Word, which is living and active; sharper than any two-edged sword.

At this moment, I choose to take upon me, your yoke, which is light and full of rest. I am grateful for this rest you provide. A rest that goes beyond mere physical relaxation and reaches deep into my soul, bringing peace and restoration. Your presence is my sanctuary, where I find comfort and rejuvenation. I declare that I am filled with the peace and joy of the Lord, which is my strength. I speak to my soul: align with my spirit, which is filled with God's Holy Spirit.

Lord, I confess that there have been times I have grown weary in doing good. Please fill me anew with Your Spirit and raise me up again. I need your enduring strength and grace to sustain me through each day. I lay all my burdens at your feet, trusting in your compassionate care. Renew my energy, Lord, and empower me to continue walking in your light and love, knowing that your strength is made perfect in my weakness.

Continue to empower me, Lord, so I can fulfill your will. Help me to keep my focus on you and not on the pain and hurt that sometimes overwhelms my heart, mind, and body. Fill me with your spirit of grace and supplication, and help me navigate victoriously through these 21 days of prayer for breakthrough.

Psalm 6:2 echoes my plea: "Be gracious to me, O Lord, for I am languishing; heal me, O Lord, for my bones are troubled." I am deeply grateful for your unwavering support and boundless grace, which empower me to stand firm even in the midst of adversity. Thank you for being my refuge and my healer, restoring both my body and my spirit.

Thank you, God, for the physical strength to fight this battle and for the spiritual fortitude to maintain my faith. Your power sustains me through every challenge, and your grace renews my spirit daily.

In Jesus' Name, I pray. Amen.

DAY 14

AFFIRMATION

I am filled with divine energy and vitality.

Day 15

GRATITUDE AND PETITION FOR CONTINUED HEALING

Heavenly Father,

Today I come before you with heart full of gratitude for your unending mercy and for the answers that I will receive concerning my prayers of restoring my health and well-being. I stand on your word in Matthew 21:22, "If you believe you will receive whatever you ask for in prayer." Thank you for never leaving nor forsaking me, for guiding me to seek you in this appointed time of dedicated prayer and breakthrough.

I am deeply thankful for your promises, as declared in Jeremiah 30:17, "But I will restore you to health and heal your wounds". Your word is a constant source of hope and strength, continually teaching me about your boundless love and the promises you freely give. I will use your promises as my anchor and your love as my guiding light, to lift my head each day and keep looking for my total healing.

Lord, as spoken in Joel 2:23, I ask you to pour out your former and latter rains upon my life—bless me abundantly and without end. I desire to give you all the glory, acknowledging your faithfulness, favor, and love as my ultimate deliverer through your supernatural power. I stand in awe of your magnificent grace and mercy.

You have made profound promises and I yearn to live in great health to witness their fulfillment and to enjoy the life you have planned for me. Hebrews 4:16 encourages me to approach your throne of grace with confidence, to receive mercy and find grace in my time of need. I stand on this promise, expecting to see the complete materialization of your word in my life.

Reminding you of 1 John 5:14-15, I hold onto the confidence that if we ask anything according to your will, you hear us. And if we know that you hear us, we can be assured that we have what we have asked of you. Thank You, Lord, for hearing my prayers and moving mountains on my behalf.

Thank you for every blessing and for the anticipation of continued healing. Mountains are moving, and your faithfulness is ever-present. I see the evidence of your power in my life, and I trust that you will continue to work miracles on my behalf.

Isaiah 53:5 says "By His stripes, we are healed". I stand firmly this day on this promise, declaring and claiming that healing right now. No illness, no affliction, no challenge is greater than your mighty hand, in Jesus' name.

Amen.

I am a living testimony of God's healing power.

Day 16

SEEKING, ASKING, KNOCKING

My Loving Father,

You said in your word, Matthew 7:7-8: "Ask and it will be given to you; seek and you will find; knock and the door will be opened to you." So I come before you this day with a hopeful heart, seeking, asking, and knocking at your door, for particular attention and care. I come seeking healing and total deliverance for my disease. I claim this promise, trusting that you have granted me this petition. I seek favorable reports from my doctors, and I thank You in advance for your favor that encompasses me as a shield.

Thank you, Father, for the assurance that your word never returns void but accomplishes what you desire and achieves the purposes for which you sent it. Today, I hold onto the promises in Matthew 7:7-11, believing that as I ask, it will be given; as I seek, I will find; as I knock, doors will be opened.

I thank you for bending your ear toward me and inclining to my cries. I am reminded of Proverbs 15:29, which assures us that you hear the prayers of the righteous. Lord, if there is anything in my life that needs reconciliation or correction, reveal it to me, Holy Spirit, that I may align fully with your will. I want to be obedient to God's word and receive favour and blessings.

Lord, I also knock on the door of salvation and deliverance from any harm, death, or loss. Open this door for me, Father, as only you can. Secure my path and guide my steps towards recovery and peace. According to Jeremiah 33:6, you have promised to bring health and healing, to let your people enjoy abundant peace and security. I stand on this promise, confident in your loving provision.

Grant me, Father, all the best gifts that align with your perfect will. Let there be no limit to your generosity, as you have promised to give good gifts to your children who ask. I am ready to receive all that you have prepared for me, knowing that every gift is a manifestation of your love and grace.

Thank you for your unfailing love and for doing all these things out of your great compassion for me. I am eternally grateful and stand in awe of your boundless mercy. I will continue to seek, ask, and knock, trusting that I will receive your healing and totally recover in your perfect time.

In Jesus' Name, I pray, Amen.

DAY 16
AFFIRMATION

I am recovering swiftly and completely.

Day 17

TRUSTING IN YOUR PROVISION AND HEALING

Merciful Father,

I come before you today with a heart full of gratitude and faith, trusting in your boundless provision and healing power. You are the great provider, and your word assures me that you will supply all my needs according to your riches in glory through Christ Jesus (Philippians 4:19). I rest in this promise, knowing that you are more than capable of meeting every need in my life.

I acknowledge, Lord, that your kingdom is not about physical nutrition alone, but is founded on righteousness, peace, and joy in the Holy Spirit (Romans 14:17). I am grateful that through Jesus, I have been made the righteous of God, and now I ask that you fill me with the fruits of Your Spirit—joy, which is my strength; your empowering peace; and the righteousness that guides my steps.

Thank You, Father, for the assurance that the same Spirit who raised Jesus from the dead lives in me. This mighty presence offers not only life but vibrant health. Proverbs 4:20-22 instructs me to attend to your words closely, for they are life and health to my entire being. I embrace this promise, believing in your word that you will raise me up and bring healing to my flesh.

Lord, help me to keep my mind steadfast on you, setting my thoughts on things above, not on earthly concerns. Strengthen my faith to walk on water, keeping my eyes fixed on you, the author and perfecter of my faith. Like the multitudes in Luke 6:19, who found healing by touching Jesus, may your healing power flow into my life. I seek to draw near to you, to touch the hem of your garment in faith, and to experience the transformative healing that only you can provide.

I humbly ask for every good and perfect gift you have prepared for me, be given to me in Jesus Name. I pray for a double portion of your blessings in every area of my life, trusting that as I seek your kingdom first, and all these things will be added unto me. May I also trust in your perfect plan and timing as I eagerly await your healing touch.

Thank you for the assurance of your kingdom and for the abundant life that you offer. I receive your gifts with a grateful heart and pledge to keep my eyes fixed on you, trusting that you are in control and that your ways are higher than my ways.

In moments of doubt or fear, remind me of your sovereignty and your unfailing love.

I pray all this in Jesus mighty name. Amen.

DAY 17
AFFIRMATION

I declare, I will receive God's healing and restoration.

Day 18

GUIDANCE AND INTERCESSION OF THE HOLY SPIRIT

Eternal Lord,

Thank You profoundly for the precious gift of the Holy Spirit, who you sent to dwell within us as a guide into all truth. I am eternally grateful for this Helper, who sustains and empowers us, following the ultimate sacrifice of Your Son, Jesus. I rely on the Holy Spirit to reveal your truths and be my constant companion, providing wisdom, comfort, and strength in every circumstance.

Lord, I ask for the Holy Spirit to work within me, restoring health to my body and vigor to my spirit. Let faith swell within me like a tide, bringing wisdom and insight into every aspect of my life, particularly this current challenge I face. I seek your revelation, Lord; open my eyes to see the spiritual realities and the plans you have laid out for me, especially those concerning my healing and well-being.

Father, elevate the plane on which I operate. Lift me from the lower realms of doubt and despair to higher places of faith and victory. Adjust my perspective, aligning it more perfectly with yours so that I might think, act, and believe as you would have me do. Holy Spirit, glorify Jesus through my life. Let Him be exalted in all things, and if there is anything within me that detracts from His glory, I pray you would gently correct and refine me.

Speak your heavenly promises into my existence, Lord, and let them not return to you void. I declare and command these promises to be made evident in my life as I trust in your word that I shall not just live but thrive abundantly after this period of illness.

Show me, Lord, the visions of what you have in store for me. For John 16:13 say "But when he, the Spirit of truth, comes, he will guide you into all the truth. He will not speak on his own; he will speak only what he hears, and he will tell you what is yet to come." May I hear the Holy Spirit oh Lord. Strengthen my faith to believe in the revelations you provide, that I might grasp them with both hands and hold on tight, even before they come to pass. Magnify your presence in my life, showcasing your power and grace.

Thank You, Father, for the unending grace and the intercession of the Holy Spirit. I am grateful for every breath and the continual guidance you provide through Your Spirit. Show me your matchless love and with your healing hands heal me and restore me to great health.

In the mighty and matchless name of Jesus, Amen.

My body is a temple of the Holy Spirit, and it is healthy.

Day 19

GRATITUDE AND ANTICIPATION
FOR GOD'S PROVISION

O God of all comfort,

Your word said in 1 Thessalonians 5:18: "Give thanks in all circumstances; for this is God's will for you in Christ Jesus." So I thank you for each trial and tribulation that I have to endure, for I know that you have woven every difficult moment into a tapestry of your grace and goodness. Each challenge will refine my faith and strengthen me, and I am profoundly grateful for your sustaining presence through it all. Lord, you have brought me to see another day, and I stand in awe of your enduring faithfulness.

I trust you wholeheartedly, loving you with all my heart, living for your purpose, and surrendering my times into your hands. Despite the trials I face, I am reminded that this battle is Yours, Lord, and you promise revival and restoration. As Psalm 107:20 says "He sent out his word and healed them; he rescued them from the grave." I do believe I will be healed and I will recover from this disease.

Holy Spirit, come from the four winds and breathe life into me so that I may live fully once again. When my words fail, I know you will intercede with groaning too deep for words, presenting my prayers to God in perfect accordance with his will (Romans 8:26-27). I am humbled and grateful for this divine assistance, knowing that every need and concern is brought before your throne with clarity and purpose.

Oh Lord, fill me with a fresh fire; let the rain of your Spirit flow into my soul, spirit, and body right now. Saturate every part of me with your divine presence, infusing me with renewed energy and purpose. Continue to fill me with your courage and strength, empowering me to press forward and live a fulfilled life according to your will and plan for me.

Thank You for roaring over me with your mighty voice, dispelling fear and uncertainty from my heart. Your powerful presence drives away all darkness and fills me with confidence. Each day, as you wake me up, you renew my hope and my faith. Your mercies are new every morning, and your faithfulness is my anchor. I am deeply grateful for the hope that sustains me, the hope that I will recover fully from this illness and be restored to perfect health.

Lord, your mercies are new every morning, and your faithfulness is my foundation. I am thankful for each breath and for the promise of a brighter, healthier future. I trust in your unfailing love and your sovereign power to heal and restore me completely.

In your Holy name I pray, Amen.

DAY 19

Healing flows through me with every breath I take.

Day 20

THANKSGIVING AND ANTICIPATION FOR GOD'S PROMISES

Merciful Father,

I come before you with a heart overflowing with gratitude for the manifold blessings you have showered upon me — you have sustained my life. I am profoundly thankful for your guidance through adversities and for delivering me from the challenges posed by my adversaries. With Your unwavering presence, I now stand on the brink of entering the Promised Land, ready to embrace the fullness of your promises.

Lord, I am reminded of your powerful words in Isaiah 55:11, declaring that your word will not return to you void but will accomplish all that you desire and achieve the purpose for which you sent it. You have promised healing, and I claim that promise today, in Jesus name, declaring and receiving your healing touch over every part of my body. You have assured us a life of abundance, and I declare and decree, that abundance is mine. I pray for your mercy to enrich and safeguard my life.

Father, I humbly ask that you accelerate the appearance of the blessings destined for my future, bringing them into my present. Reveal to me the extent of health and prosperity I can achieve. I pray for a thousand-fold increase in every good thing—enhance my vitality and fortify my body's cells with strength to triumph in every challenge. For you alone oh God can speak to every fiber of my being and command them to function and heal me.

Lord, let this day be marked by the visible signs of your responses to my prayers. I thank you in advance for the blessings multiplied, as promised in Deuteronomy 1:11. May my journey be a testament to your faithfulness, walking by faith and bolstered by the tangible evidence of your hand at work in my life.

Thank you Father, for the assurance of your promises and the endless support of your love and mercy. I put on the belt of truth, the breastplate of righteousness, the shoes of the gospel of peace, the shield of faith, the helmet of salvation, and the sword of the Spirit, which is your word (Ephesians 6:14-17). May I continually walk in your grace and experience the reality of your divine provision and total restoration.

I declare healing is my portion in the mighty name of Jesus,
Amen.

DAY 20

AFFIRMATION

My spirit is resilient, and I am overcoming all challenges.

Day 21

CELEBRATION OF GOD'S FAITHFULNESS

My Lord and Savior,

I stand in awe of you and the marvelous works you perform. "Blessed be Your Name, Lord God Almighty Forever!" I celebrate your name and the wondrous deeds you have accomplished in my life, particularly over these past 21 days of devoted prayer. Your word has been my anchor, your love my refuge and your power my strength.

Lord, thank You for the journey we have walked together. Your presence has been a constant assurance and comfort. You know me intimately, so I place my complete trust in your divine plans. As you said in Proverbs 3:5-6: "Trust in the Lord with all your heart and lean not on your own understanding; in all your ways submit to him, and he will make your paths straight." I trust you and thank you in advance for using me to be a living testament and prove your might and miracles.

As I walk in your victory and power, I surrender all glory to you. Continue to guide my steps, for they are ordered by you. I now you are refining me as you make all things beautiful in your design and in your time. This will definitely be a journey of faith, even as my physical body is experiencing turmoil; I believe you are shaping me into a living testimony of your grace and mercy. So I have faith that I will be healed. I know you can do immeasurably more than all I can ever ask or imagine, according to the power that works within us." Ephesians 3:20

Thank You for the exceptional medical team you have placed in my path, whose skills and dedication will be a source of favor and healing. May any surgeries that are to be perform may they be done with great excellence and may I have a speedy recovery. I am also thanking you in advance for the efficacy of each treatment I am to receive. I am confident that every medicine works to restore and heal me to perfect health, as you have ordained.

Oh God and I as go through this journey I ask you to renew my heart and mind, teach me the grace of forgiveness and fortify my spirit with your peace and wisdom. Above all, on the last day of my prayer and fast I want to thank you and declare that I am entirely grateful for all you have done and about to do in my life. I worship you and I celebrate your faithfulness and the healing you will bestow upon my body, in the mighty name of Jesus.

As I continue to trust you without reservation, I rely not on my own understanding but on your word, your infinite wisdom and your boundless love.

In Jesus name I pray, Amen.

DAY 21

I am healed by the stripes of Jesus.

My Journal

Day 1 – Dear Lord I ask you to walk with me through this. Show me you are here.

Dear Lord I ask you to slay the works of the enemy. And restore my health. In Jesus Name

Dear Lord I trust that I have a wonderful future ahead of me. Open before me double doors

Dear Lord release abundant blessings over me. Isaiah 45:1-8

Dear Father I ask for your promise of Psalm 32 - Instruct me & teach me in the way you should go, & guide me with your eye upon me. Order my steps oh God, by your will today & forever. Jeremiah 14:6?

Dear God I repent for every time that I've insisted on my own whole plan before I take the first step of faith into the unknown.

Matthew 6:33 Seek 1st the Kingdom of God and his

I pray you bless my life and protect it, h, h, T, h... I ask my Father that you pull good things that was originally intended for my future into my present right now.

Dear Lord give me a thousand fold increase of good things and increase my good need & will to bless others. Fill them with oxygen that they are super strong to fight the good fight

---

Dear Lord I confess to you today any way I have been weary in well doing. I ask you to fill me, oh God, with your Spirit and raise me up again.

Verbally command strength into You Spirit

- "I command strength into my body, soul & spirit in Jesus Name! I am filled with the peace & joy oh Lord, which is

---

Day 2 – Dear Lord I fall under the covenant you made with Abraham so I have all the covenant promises and privileges that You promised /made/paid to?

Dear Lord, I need your help in this situation and my help and healing comes from you alone. Deliver me.

Dear Lord or your Al... result I beg you do not put me to shame. Save

---

Dear Lord I confess to you today any way I have been weary in well doing. I ask you to fill me, oh God, with your Spirit and raise me up again. Verbally command strength into Your spirit - "I command strength into my body, soul & spirit in Jesus Name! I am filled with the peace & joy of Lord, which is

---

I ask for great health this day, supernatural healing. Fill me with your peace and power.

Dear Father make me blessable - say & be right with you and obedient to you in every area of my life.

Dear Heavenly Father my provider, bring me a godly harvest, good work results and favor right now in the same

---

Day 3 – Dear God I trust and know you are still the front I am & Lord over all. As attacked in 2 Corinthians 12:9 the Power of Christ rest upon me. Thank you for your grace by which I am saved.

Dear Lord, I thank you for your active grace in my life that helps me everyday even when I don't notice.

Fill me with fresh fire of God & let the Rain of Your spirit pour into my spirit, soul and body right now. Continue to fill me with your courage & strength.

Thank you for watching over me.

Thank you for filling me with peace, joy & power.

Thank You Lord for waking me up filled with more life than I have ever had.

Dear God bless me & enlarge my territory, keep

Day 6 – Father God help me dwell in the secret place of the Most High, in your presence as you said in your word (Psalm 91:1)

Help me oh God to abide in the shadow of the Almighty (Psalm 91:1)

Dear God you are my refuge and fortress in you I trust.

Thank You Father for giving your angels charge

Protect me from the enemy and teach me to see my salvation that you will accomplish today.

Exodus 14:13-14 I will see him sixteen no more forever.

Father God fill me with perfect love so I will not be afraid.

Dear Lord I rest in you & ask. I ask you to lift me up as well, since I can do nothing without - but you can do all

---

Dear Father I remind you 1 John 5:14-15, "And this is the confidence that we have in him, that if we ask anything according to your will, He hear us. And if we know that You hear us, whatever we ask, we know that we have petitions that we have asked of You God.

Thank You Lord for hearing my prayers. Thanks Holy Spirit for helping my prayer. And thank you for giving me the petitions asked

---

Bring me comfort and encouragement in every situation in my life, every moment of the day.

Thank You Lord God, my daddy, for increasing me & comforting me & using my life as your playground for pouring out your goodness on this earth.

Thank you for blessing me & taking care of me as well, and I give you all the glory, honor and praise

Author Bio

My story is one of resilience, faith, and miraculous healing. In October 2019, my life took an unexpected turn when I was diagnosed with a rare form of cancer, acinic cell carcinoma of the maxillary sinus. The news was earth-shattering, and I was immediately thrust into a whirlwind of medical appointments, treatments, and surgeries.

The journey was arduous. Chemotherapy sessions left me physically and emotionally drained, and multiple surgeries tested my strength. There were days when the pain and fear felt overwhelming, but I found solace in my faith. Prayer became my anchor, providing a source of comfort and hope. I believed that God was with me through every challenge, guiding me and giving me the strength to keep fighting.

Today, I am proud to say that I am a cancer survivor. My battle with cancer has not only strengthened my faith but has also brought incredible joy and blessings into my life. The man who stood by my side through every painful step of this journey is now my loving husband. Together, despite the predictions the doctors gave, that chemotherapy would render me unable to conceive within a year after my last treatment. We have defied the odds and have been blessed with our beautiful, healthy daughter. This miracle is a testament to God's mercy and favor.

The experience of surviving cancer and witnessing such profound blessings inspired me to write a 21-day prayer book for healing and recovery. This book is a collection of prayers that helped me through my darkest days, and it is my hope that these prayers will offer comfort and strength to others facing their own battles. Through prayer, I found the courage to endure, the faith to believe in miracles, and the peace to accept God's plan for my life.

Writing this book has been a deeply personal journey, one that has allowed me to reflect on the incredible support I received from my family, friends, and faith community. Their unwavering love and encouragement were vital to my recovery, and I am eternally grateful.

Thank you for taking the time to read my story. It is my sincere hope that my journey and this prayer book will be a source of hope and healing for anyone facing difficult times. Remember, with faith, anything is possible.

With gratitude and blessings,
Kay M. Forde

Printed in the United States
by Baker & Taylor Publisher Services